BOOK TITLE

THE AMAZING PARENT

SUBTITLE

HOW TO RAISE KIDS TO BECOME GENIUSES: THE GOD'S WAY

AUTHORS NAME
STELLAR DONALD

COPYRIGHT
All rights reserved...

TABLE OF CONTENTS

Chapter 5: The hard skills for parenting

Chapter 6:Where to Find Good Parenting Information

Chapter 7: The Advantages of Good Parenting strategies

Chapter 8: The A-Z of parenting advice, tips, and secrets

Chapter 9: The strategies for becoming an exceptional parent.

Introduction

Good parenting entails a high level of consistency and routine, which provides children with a sense of control. Redundancy becomes the goal for parents as good parenting focuses on developing independence in children. A good parenting style takes into account the age and stage of development of the child. Great parents prioritize their children's health and well-being.

Nurturing the whole child entails attending to physical, mental, social, emotional, and intellectual needs. The role of a parent is therefore a tedious one and parents must make time to show up for their child from time to time.

Basics

Children are God's gift to parents, they bring joy and pride to the aged and everyone around. Psalms 127:3 says that children are a heritage from God and a reward from him. This shows that every child comes from God and belongs to God.

The role of a parent can therefore be likened to that of a caretaker, a nurturer, and an overseer. The Bible teaches parents to diligently bring up their kids in the ways of the lord. Sometimes Dad and Mom get so busy that they don't have free time for their kids, but even with your tight schedule, you have to make time for your kids. You can employ the services of a home teacher, or a nanny or be available to them during your free time. Engage them in fun activities like gaming, word search, and educational and spiritual TV shows, and always teach them to pray and read the scriptures to them.

With our technology today, they are perfectly capable of learning on their own. Also, by doing small things such as reading for them, you will prepare them for a brighter future. Why not go over the words with them or point them out to objects and have them sound them out? You'd be surprised by what they can learn.

You must stay calm with them while teaching. This experience should be fun for them so don't let it seem like work. If they don't understand something, you can move on to the next subject. Toddlers or kids will easily become bored with the same subject.

Some parents will raise their tone when teaching a child and we suggest that you don't do this. You should never become frustrated if they cannot learn something. Instead, taking your time and going a different route is better. Toddlers and kids are extremely sensitive and this is why you should always have patience with them.

Once your child goes to their first day of kindergarten, you won't have to worry about them falling behind. They will be ready to conquer the world and the teacher will be impressed with what they can do.

By making educational choices for your children, you can leave a good impression as a parent. Generally, educationally inclined kids will have an easier time socializing and communicating with other kids. This means that they'll be able to make a few good friends and won't be lonely in their class.

For most parents, this is very important. Life is all about communicating with others. Parents should always instill godly values and lessons they have learned in their kids. Encourage them to have godly friends as well, in the church, and school, and neighborhood, teach them the dangers of keeping bad company

Chapter 1:
The Fundamentals of child-rearing

Raising kids is not just fun and play, it requires effort from both parents. You must teach them manners, discipline, and respect as well. Most kids don't want to learn these things but to be a good parent, you should teach them everything they need to know about life.

Remember that you should always begin when the child is young. We recommend starting lessons for them when they are a toddler. You aren't going to jump ahead 4 grades and start teaching them advanced math. Their brain is still developing and they are still learning speech plus basic movement skills. With this in mind, you'll need to raise your kids by giving them simple activities that have to do with colors, hand-eye coordination, and memorization. These are the most basic skills a child will need in life. By dealing with these skills first, they'll be confident to learn a lot more.

Behind The Scenes

If your child seems rebellious or against the thought of learning about certain subjects, you'll need to motivate them. What is it that your child enjoys? Do they have a certain activity or something that they want? If so, you should act on whatever that is. For example, if they love eating cookies and you rarely give them cookies, it is a good idea to reward them. You can reward them for completing tasks just by giving them cookies. They will look forward to their next task because they know if they complete it- they will get another cookie. This way it is like a fun game for them.

When it comes to raising kids, you should always organize everything accordingly. Wake them up at the same time for their breakfast and start their toddler lessons at noon. The reason why we do this is so that they can get used to their schedule. If you jumble everything up, they may not be in the mood to learn. Believe it or not, some toddlers develop a feel for "time". If they normally eat and study after - they will be prepared for this.

Also, this will allow you to relax and stop worrying about if they will take part in your lessons or not. They won't say no since they already know the time has come to learn. Eventually, they will get used to it.

"Train up a child in the way he should go; even when he is old he will not depart from it." -Proverbs 22 vs 6.

"I have no greater joy than to hear that my children are walking in the truth."- 3 John 1:4

One of your greatest weapons as parents is prayers to God. Ask God for the wisdom to raise your children in good manners and values pleasing unto him.

Chapter 2:

A GENIUS'S CHARACTERISTICS

A genius is someone smart, and logical observes what's going on around them, and is a problem solver. If you want them to become geniuses, it will take hard work.

However, this doesn't mean you need to take two hours out of your day to teach your children. A brief lesson is fine and would be better for the child. You don't want to drag the lesson on for so long that they eventually don't want to participate anymore. A lesson should last for 10-30 minutes only, depending on how young they are. If you want your kid to become a genius, you'll need to pay attention to their progress.

Here are a few characteristics of a genius below:

The Signs

Logical

A genius thinks logically and can connect two seemingly unrelated ideas to conclude. Assume you have some educational flashcards for your child. They are given four learning cards and are required to identify which object does not belong. There are three different types of birds and one car on one of the cards. A logical child will choose the car because it does not resemble the birds.

Observing

You will notice that your child responds to sounds and visuals in their environment if they are observing. Determine the number of calls you must make before your child responds. It's a good idea to work on this if they arrive in five minutes. When they arrive, give them a prize. This will aid the situation.

Examine your child to see if he or she responds more to sounds or visuals. If they appear to prefer visuals more frequently, this indicates that they are a visual learner. Visual learners frequently become artists later in life, but there are other professions as well.

Smart

A smart child will start talking at a young age and will even give proper nouns to objects. If you have a younger toddler who is still learning the names of objects, - You might be able to assist them. Point to each item and tell them what it is. Only do this with three items at a time to ensure that it sticks in their minds.

Learning too much too soon can cause the child to become confused, and they may even get their words mixed up. To do it. Children who can retain certain information are naturally smart, and by capitalizing on this, they can go a long way. Work with their strengths while also assisting them with areas of difficulty.

"All your children shall be taught by the Lord, and great shall be the peace of your children."-Isaiah 54vs 13

"Before I formed you in the womb I knew you, and before you were born I consecrated you; I appointed you a prophet to the nations." -Jeremiah 1:5

Every child is created with distinct capabilities and talents, no one knows your child more than the creator. Trust him in helping you bring up your child.

Chapter 3:

How to transform your kids to become geniuses.

You will need to devise a strategy to transform your children into geniuses. Make a list of the materials you will need to teach them.

First, determine whether they are a visual or hands-on learner. This way, you can give them an advantage when learning. You want the process to be simple for them; otherwise, they may be less enthusiastic about learning. This has a negative impact and will prevent them from progressing in their education. Play some games with your kids.

Synopsis

There are two symbols on the ball. On the ball, you can tape a butterfly and a dog. Request that they pass you the ball containing the dog. Repeat this several times so that they can learn identification skills as well as nouns.

It is also a good idea to go to a store in your area and look for educational toys. Make certain that the toys are both safe and age-appropriate. If you have a two-year-old, you should not be teaching them things that a six-year-old would know.

You can pay a year or two, but no further. Numerous games can be created or purchased. Mini computer games, word games, symbol games, geometrical games, and so on are available. Feel free to let them choose which game to play. This should be repeated several times so that they can learn identification skills as well as nouns. If your child is young, you'll need to choose for them.

- ***Invest in technology that makes a difference.***

This means that you should buy technology that teaches them to speak and type. This may be a big step for them, and you can either wait until they are older or start now. For example, consider purchasing a piano with picture-based keys.

The piano will inquire as to the location of the various animals on the keys. A happy song is played if they get it right. If it is incorrect, the answer is revealed. Aside from a piano, you could get a high-tech child's computer that pronounces new words and allows them to type them. They can find the letter on the keyboard and practice typing right away... Before you know it, they will be ahead of their class.

- ***Make daily activities a part of your daily learning process.***

You can continue teaching them even after education time has ended and lunch has begun. Inquire about the type of cereal they're eating, the color of the cereal, or the name of the utensils they're using. If they are very young and are unable to tell you everything, simply repeat it.

Hold up the object you are discussing while repeating the answer. Make it enjoyable for them by sticking to the same topic each week. We say for a week so that they can remember the information. The following week, you can switch it up and do learning with a different daily activity.

"For I know the plans I have for you," declares the Lord, "plans to prosper you and not to harm you, plans to give you hope and a future"-Jeremiah 29:11 (NIV)

"grow in the grace and knowledge of our Lord and Savior Jesus Christ"-2 Peter 3:18 (NKJV)

Chapter 4:
The soft skills needed for effective parenting

Synopsis

Gentle discipline, Patience, understanding, comfort, and love are the foundations of good parenting. If you give your child everything they need in a balanced manner, they will have no negative feelings about their past. Many children miss out on a few things as they grow up.

Either the parent is too soft to show them the rules, or they are unable to express their love. For example, a father may always bring his son to baseball practice, but he never compliments him on his performance. Instead, he yells at him all the time and tells him he could have done better. His son grows up without love or understanding. This is because he was so young that he did not understand his father's reasoning. Men will often show their love differently and some kids do not understand this which transforms into anger or sadness once they look at their past.

Soft Skill

What about a mother who lavishes her child with affection? She has a big heart and will practically do anything for her daughter. What she is doing is making life easier for herself, but this will not work. To obtain things, you must work hard. When it comes to balancing everything out, there is a distinction. You are preparing your daughter for failure in life if she does not learn discipline.

She will continue to break rules and will eventually rebel in social situations or at work. Instead, striking a balance between everything is a good idea. With balance, you consider all of the soft skills required for good parenting. If you don't balance everything, your child will become obsessed with a single goal in life. They won't be good at anything else. What if your child only plays basketball and ignores their schoolwork? This can be devastating if your child breaks their leg during a game one day. They are almost certainly not going to be able to play again.

Check to see if they are knowledgeable in a variety of areas. By doing so, you are giving them a lot of options in life. They could become a graphic artist or an architect-planner. There are numerous options available, and you must focus on what they are good at while also strengthening the skills they require assistance with. Many parents are unaware that they are making this mistake. By starting this early, your child will flourish in life.

For most parents, comfort and understanding go hand in hand. If your son is having difficulty making friends in his second-grade class, you will naturally want to console him. This is something that every parent should do. If you do not provide comfort to your children, they will become lonely and even upset. They will feel hopeless, and they will wish you had paid more attention to them. Even if you have never been in their situation, it is still a good idea to console them. Tell your children that everything will be fine and that you will always be there for them.

When they are faced with a difficult situation, they will look up to you and run. The human mind is very strong and some kids can even remember things from back to when they were five months old - even if it was just a blurry memory.

"And you, fathers, do not provoke your children to wrath, but bring them up in the training and admonition of the Lord"- Ephesians 6:4

Chapter 5:
The hard skills for parenting

Synopsis

Hard parenting skills are critical for your child, especially in their early years. Strictness, tough love, and self-soothing are examples of hard skills. No parent wants to be perceived as the bad guy in the relationship, which is why we are less strict these days. It's not like it was 60 years ago when children were frequently hit and scolded for doing things we now consider "innocent."

However, if you want your child to grow up strong, you will need to work on a few hard parenting skills. If you don't want to be perceived as the bad guy, why not share the hard skills with your spouse? Most of the time, When the father is overly lenient and the mother is overly strict, the child will run to the father. Because the mother says no, the father may argue with her, causing problems in the relationship. This also demonstrates to the child that whatever they do is acceptable.

They are perplexed because one parent allows them to do something and the other does not. To avoid confusion, talk with your significant other and make decisions together.

Hard abilities

Don't be an enabler by letting them do whatever they want. If you have a nine-month-old baby who frequently cries to get what they want, you might rush over to comfort them. They will eventually need to learn to talk instead of crying. This is why we invented the concept of "self-soothing." Instead of constantly comforting your child, you should allow them some alone time.

You should put them in their crib if you've tried everything and they've been crying for hours. Before you do this, make sure they don't have any medical issues. Close the door and let them cry after you've placed them. It may break your heart to hear them cry, but they will need to understand that crying does not always elicit a response. You will notice that they are crying less, and as you teach them speech, they will begin to rely on this for communication.

In another case, you have a three-year-old who is always running around the house and saying "no" to you. This is a normal developmental stage that many children go through. They believe that by saying "no," they will avoid having to do things like eat vegetables or take a bath.

At this point, you'll have to show them some tough love. This means that if they push their food away and refuse to eat, they should just leave it alone. If they see someone in the family eating cookies and want some, tell them calmly that they must first finish their dinner.

By not making a big deal out of it, your child will not feel pressured to do things they don't want to. Place the saved dinner in front of them. If they eat it, give them a cookie as a reward. This is a great way to be firm while still giving them what they want.

Chapter 6:

Where to find good parenting information

Synopsis

Those who have an iPod or iPhone would benefit greatly from this and you'll even be able to take your book on the road. Tired of sitting through long office meetings? Continue reading from where you left off. This is one of the reasons we appreciate modern technology. You no longer need to go to the library to borrow books. Everything you need is right in front of your eyes.

If you frequent the library, you will find a wealth of information on how you can help your child become smarter than everyone else in the class. You will succeed in your child's learning abilities if you devote so much time to them during the school day. It just takes a lot of perseverance and devotion. Keep in mind that if you are looking for something specific that you will have to conduct a search. Use your search query online. If your baby has been crying for hours and you just don't know what to do, you can read up on skills to comfort your little one.

Learning new parenting skills is simple, and with so much information available, you can almost find anything. However, if you are having difficulty deciding which product to purchase, you must first identify your needs. Before you buy an ebook, see if you can read the table of contents. This will give you an idea of what the book is about, and you will avoid purchasing something that already contains the information you are familiar with.

Some e-books include excerpts that highlight the main points of the book. This is a good book to read if you've never bought anything from the author before and aren't sure what to expect. Make a note of any useful information you come across. Make notes about what you're reading so you'll remember it when the time comes.

Chapter 7:

Advantages of good parenting

Synopsis

Good parenting can help your child grow into a self-assured, happy, and intelligent adult who knows what they want in life. Even small things you teach them can have a big impact. You may want to keep your child all to yourself and never let them grow up, but they will eventually have to make their own decisions.

Many parents find it difficult to let go of their children, but you must remember that everything you have taught them in life will only make the process easier for them. If you have worked hard to get them ahead of the other kids in school, there is a good chance they will excel in college at an early age. Once they complete college, they will be able to start looking for work and have a fulfilling life. Here are some benefits of good parenting:

The Advantages

•Confidence

You can boost your child's confidence by communicating with them daily and praising them for the good things they do. Parents who yell at their children for everything they do wrong will lower their self-esteem, having the opposite effect. Even when they are at their worst, maintain your cool.

 If your child draws on the wall, look at them with a disapproving nod and say, "No." Explain to them that this is not acceptable. Inform them that they will not be receiving dessert as a result of their actions. This produces the same reaction to what they did, but without harsh reprimand. They will be mentally healthy and self-assured.

• *Happiness*

Did you know that laughter is strongly linked to happiness? Little things like tickling your child, giving them playful kisses, or even watching cartoons with them will help to create a happy environment. They will tend to focus on positive outcomes rather than negative outcomes in life, which will make them happy. Even if your child is acting out, try to make them laugh a few times a day. If you are too stressed or simply not in the mood, do something that will make both of you happy.

• *Harmony*

If someone constantly yells and is angry in the house, you should remove them from the situation. A peaceful environment will allow your child to be happy and not be afraid to be themselves. If you suspect that your child is being abused, act quickly! It can easily scar them in the future and cause anxiety.

You may have to file an investigation report, but consider this: your child is worth it. They are the people you will be spending the next 18 years of your life with. After that, they'll most likely move on and start their own lives. But don't worry, they'll still need you and regard you as their dear mother or father.

Your job is to only give them the best in life and teach them what is right and wrong. You will allow them to grow and they will be much happier as a result. Nothing beats having a bubbly child in your life.

"Oh, that their hearts would be inclined to fear me and keep all my commands always, so that it might go well with them and their children forever!"
-Deuteronomy 5:29

Chapter 8:

The A-Z of parenting advice, tips, and secrets

Synopsis

Here is a list of A-Z parenting tips and secrets.

Tips

•Appreciation

Appreciating some of your child's accomplishments is a great way to show them you care and are proud of them.

When a child engages in positive activities, they must be recognized. If they drag your purse across hug them it's dirty in the process, simply say "thank you" and hug them. Don't chastise them for getting dirty. They are too young to understand and thought they were doing something good.

•*Comfort*

When your child is sad, lonely, or uncertain, he or she may require comfort. At 2 a.m., it was raining outside and thunder could be heard shaking the house. When your child screamed, you dashed to her aid. She was sitting up, sobbing, and unable to sleep due to the noise. Don't simply tell her to go to bed. Tell her a bedtime story and pat her on the head. Explain to her that she should not be afraid of thunder. She will eventually calm down and fall asleep.

•*Devotion*

Make the most of the time you do have by devoting it to your son or daughter. Missing them growing up may cause you to regret your work, and you may spend days wondering why time flew by so quickly.

•*Empathy*

If you have a young son who feels as if no one understands him, you should take your time figuring out what he is going through. This will be a difficult experience if you are going through a divorce with your husband and he is constantly crying for his father to come home. Rather than becoming upset and telling him to stop crying, try to explain everything to him in a gentle manner. Tell your six-year-old son that adults don't always stay together, but that doesn't mean he won't see his father. Cuddle him and tell him a soothing story to help him relax. He'll realize it as he gets older.

•Guiding

It is critical to guide your child through their education, especially if you intend to home-school them. In addition, guiding can be used for simple things like teaching your child how to eat, saying his or her name, and interacting with others.

Always demonstrate the proper procedure.

•*Nurturing*

Every child requires nurturing. Hold your child close when they are struggling in the home-school situation, and assure them that everything will be fine. They constantly look up to you and consider you a role model. Your child will be less anxious in the future if you nurture them.

• *Good Role Model*

Every child watches what their parents do and learns from them. One of the secrets of becoming a great parent is to act by doing. Teach them prayers by praying, teach giving by giving to other people, and teach care, love, and kindness by practicing them genuinely.

•*Be Friendly*

Talk with your child and help their brain integrate. Have conversations with them, and be their friend. Kids love to express themselves, join them in their extracurricular activities, and play with them, That way they will be able to open up to you about anything

•*Discipline*

Do not spank no matter what, spanking can bring short-term relief to you but it doesn't teach the difference between right from wrong, it will only make your child have fear, you should use other forms of discipline to correct the kids, and this should be done from a place of love. You don't want your child to fear you, instead, you want him to listen.

- ***Love***
- ***Prayers***
- ***Reading the scriptures as a family***

Chapter 9:
The strategies for becoming an exceptional parent

To become an exceptional parent, you must implement all of the strategies taught in this ebook. If you only concentrate on one aspect, you will not be able to balance everything out. Your child requires balance to develop into a little genius that will help him blossom early. Your child will need to learn the fundamentals of life.

If your child is a rebel who constantly says no, you must be strict with the rules. However, do not constantly hover around them. Just keep an eye on them and make sure to correct them if they make a mistake. Giving your child a head start in life is another strategy that will help you become a strong parent. You want them to be able to do things on their own, so why not start teaching them young? Instead of starting them at the age of three, start them at the age of two. You'll be happy you did. You won't have them constantly relying on you for minor tasks that they can complete on their own.

Allow your child to learn new things every day. Don't limit yourself to one lesson at a time. Why not read their stories online or purchase a new learning game for them? They'll be ecstatic and eager to get started. If they are misbehaving, try giving them a time-out.

In this day and age, spanking or any form of abuse is frowned upon. It can also severely harm a child, and they will remember it as they grow older. Most children do not understand what is right and wrong, so you must be gentle with them while reminding them of the proper behavior.

What is the Bible's take on parenting?
Not all parents are aware of the beauty of a Christian family because of the homes they were raised. Some of us were raised in healthy, loving, Christ-centered homes, while others were raised in broken homes or broken situations where we experienced more pain and sadness than joy. We are free and equipped, regardless of our past, to set the tone for our family

and raise our children in a Godly environment. Your past and upbringing do not matter, everything you will ever need is in his word and we have the Holy Spirit to teach and guide us always.

The Bible depicts every type of parent, from the best to the worst. From well-known accounts of people's lives like Abraham, Jacob, David, and others, we see these believers, known for their powerful faith, make wonderful decisions, only to turn around and make terrible parenting decisions. When this happens, we must remember that we are the best parents our children could have! They are a priceless gift that God has entrusted to us in his generosity, wisdom, and providence,!

The Bible also demonstrates that each child is unique, no child is the same. Every child has a distinct attribute carved by God. Jacob and Esau were distinct, and Cain and Abel were also distinct. The Children of Noah are also distinct and different from one another. This was fine, and it was all part of God's plan. Even with consistent parenting, our children will react differently to discipline and encouragement than their siblings.

Some children can be brought into line with a stern look or a head shake. Others require more to learn what is correct. Parents should spend a significant amount of time praying for each of their children, and most importantly, parents must seek God in their own lives so that this shines through in everything they do.

Every day, those kids are watching and learning from you, parents!

"Train up a child in the way he should go, Even when he is old he will not depart from it".-Proverbs 22:6

www.ingramcontent.com/pod-product-compliance
Lightning Source LLC
Chambersburg PA
CBHW082102130726
48003CB00009BA/2966